MICROSERVICES PATTERNS

Your Complete Handbook on Building Testable, Scalable, and Maintainable Microservices

Austin Young

Copyright@2019

Table of Contents

Introduction

The traditional way of developing enterprise applications—utilizing a monolithic method—has gotten problematic as applications become larger and more complex. Therefore, developers are moving towards microservices software development architecture, wherein applications are structured as groups of loosely coupled services. Making it easier to build, scale and expand applications.

It is not a new concept to split applications into smaller parts; there are other programming standards that address this same concept. Service Oriented Architecture (SOA) is one example of such. However, recent technology advances as well as an increasing expectation of cohesive digital experiences have led to a new variety of development techniques and tools that are used to meet the requirements of modern enterprise applications. Microservices depend not only on the technology being configured to support this approach, but also on a company having the right structure, knowledge, and culture in place for easy adoption of this concept by teams within the company. In IT departments, microservices are one part of a larger move to a DevOps culture, wherein operations and development teams collaborate closely to support an application throughout its lifecycle, and undergo a rapid or even continual release cycle instead of a more conventional long cycle.

This book attempts to examine all you need to understand regarding microservice architecture and patterns. It will help you to make knowledgeable decisions, if you plan to implement a microservice architecture.

Chapter 1

Monolithic Architecture

This can be viewed as a big container within which all of an application's components are combined and tightly packaged. These components include APIs, plugins, services, data access objects, controllers, models, and views.

Traditionally, software developers created huge, monolithic applications. One monolith would contain every code for every business activity performed by an application. As the application's requirements increased, naturally, so did the monolith. If an application becomes successful, users will like it and depend more on it; traffic will dramatically increase; and almost unavoidably, users will make requests for additional features and improvements, so more developers are brought in to support the growing application. After a while, the previously simple application becomes complex and large, having several independent development teams working on it simultaneously. However, these supposed independent teams are not actually independent whatsoever. They are concurrently working on the same codebase and concurrently changing the same segments of code. If there are multiple overlapping independent development teams working on an application, it gets virtually impossible to find out who is working on certain tasks, code quality suffers, and code changes collide. It becomes more difficult for these teams to make updates without calculating how it will impact other teams. This generally results in less-reliable, slower applications, as well as time-consuming development schedules. The consequences does not just affect the technical teams: if it is an essential application to the business, crashes, poor application performance, and development delays can end up costing the company money and customers. Fortunately, this scenario is avoidable. The applications can be redesigned and rebuilt to scale with the company's needs, and not against them. Utilizing a modern, microservices-based application framework is an increasingly popular practice for developing applications that are able to scale without entangling the company in monolithic issues.

Challenges of a Monolithic Architecture
Below are additional challenges of monolithic architecture:

- Not scalable. Monolithic applications can be hard to scale when various modules have varying resource requirements. For instance, one module might execute logic for CPU-intensive image processing and would ideally be implemented using the Compute-Optimized instances of Amazon EC2 framework. Another module could be an in-memory database that is most appropriate for EC2 Memory-Optimized instances. Since these modules are deployed at the same time, you have to make a concession on the hardware selected.

- Not suitable for complex applications. Components of complex applications contain tightly coupled dependencies.

- Slow development. It takes a lot of time to develop applications using the monolithic approach, since each component has to be built consecutively.

- Undependable. Since all modules are running in the same process, an issue in any module, for example a memory leak, can possibly bring down the whole process. Besides, since the application's instances are identical, that issue will affect the availability of the whole application.

- Blocks continuous development. Several components of an application cannot be developed and deployed simultaneously.
- Inflexible. Monolithic applications make it very hard to adopt new languages and frameworks.

Microservices

A microservice is a self-contained, small piece of code that implements a business function. It contains private data and has a clear interface. It is decoupled and simply deployed from inside a container to all environments. A microservice architecture refers to a group of loosely coupled microservices, which execute a larger collection of business functions. This is the existing standard for developing cloud-native and cloud-based applications. The term utilized for this form of solution is known as cloud microservices. Microservices are simple to continuously test, deploy, and integrate—plus software development teams can update each one independently. Microservices work in multiple environments ranging from data centers to server-less cloud computing. This approach values the ability to share same process across several applications, granularity, and being lightweight.

Microservices solve the challenges of monolithic applications by being modular. In the simplest form, microservices assists in building an application as a set of small services, with each service being independently deployable and operating in its own process. These services are designed to serve only one particular business function, such as: social media logins, search engine, e-commerce cart, user roles, user management etc. They can use different data storages and can be written in several programming languages. Microservices make use of lightweight HTTP, Thrift APIs or REST for communication.

Monolith vs Microservices

Microservices	Monolithic Architecture
More hardware resources can be allocated to frequently used services.	It is challenging and wasteful to scale applications.
It is easy to isolate issues. Even if one service fails, others can still continue to function.	It is difficult to isolate issues. If any specific component is not working, the entire system goes down. To handle this problem, the

Microservices	Monolithic Architecture
	application have to be rebuilt, retested and redeployed.
There are no cross-dependencies between codebases. You can utilize different technologies for several microservices.	One program or function depends on others.
Data is federated, thus allowing each microservice to implement a data model that best suits its needs.	The data is centralized.

Microservices	Monolithic Architecture
Every component of the whole application should be small, and be capable of delivering one specific business goal.	It has a single codebase for all business goals.
Centers on product, and not projects.	Emphasis is on the entire project.
Service startup is relatively fast.	It takes more time to start services.
Updating the data model of a single microservice does not influence other microservices.	Any change in data model impacts the entire database.
All microservices are loosely coupled. Hence, changes made	Monolithic architecture is tightly coupled. Any

Microservices	Monolithic Architecture
in one service have no effect on the other services.	change in a single module will affect the rest.
Parallel and faster development. Small focused teams.	Large team and significant team management effort is needed.
Microservices are continuously available and always remain consistent.	Development tools become overburdened, as the process have to start from scratch.
Businesses can set up more resources for services that are producing higher return-on-investment.	Individual resource allocation is not possible seeing that services are not isolated.

Microservices	Monolithic Architecture
Communicates with other microservices by making use of well-defined interfaces.	Not applicable.

Characteristics of Microservices

Applications built using microservices have certain characteristics. These include:

- *Specialized*: each service is built for a specific set of capabilities with focus on resolving a specific issue. If developers contribute additional code to a service for a while and the service gets complex, it can be separated into smaller services.

- *Autonomous*: each component within a microservice architecture can be scaled, operated, deployed, and developed without affecting the functionality of other components. Services do not have to share their implementation or code with other services. All communication between individual components occurs through well-defined APIs.

- **Decentralized Governance**: the focus here is on using the appropriate tool for the appropriate job. Meaning that there is no technology pattern or standardized pattern. Developers are free to choose the best beneficial tools to solve their issues. Teams building microservices usually prefer a different tactic to standards. Instead of using a set of established standards, they prefer the notion of producing functional tools that can be used by other developers to solve issues similar to those they are tackling. These tools are usually gathered from implementations and then shared with a broader group, sometimes, (but not specifically) using an internal open-source model.

- **Responsibility**: microservices do not treat applications as projects. Rather, applications are regarded as products that they are responsible for. The product approach ties in with the relationship to business capabilities. Instead of regarding the software as a collection of functionalities to be accomplished, there is an ongoing relationship that involves the question of how software can assist its users to improve the business capability. There is no reason why this approach cannot be used on monolithic applications, but the reduced granularity of services makes it easier to build the personal relationships between users and service developers.

- **Continuous Delivery**: allows frequent software releases, through efficient automation of software development, testing, and approval.

- *Decoupling*: services within the application are largely decoupled. Allowing the application to be easily scaled, altered and built.
- *Encapsulation*: services encapsulate internal implementation details. This way, external systems that make use of the services do not have to be concerned about the internals. Encapsulation minimizes the complexity and improves the flexibility of the system.
- Microservice applications can be distributed across data centers and clouds.

Advantages of Microservices

Microservices offer companies many advantages, these include:

- The microservices architecture pattern allows the independent scaling of each service. You can deploy the right amount of instances per service that satisfy its availability and capacity constraints. Moreover, you can make use of the hardware that is most appropriate for the resource requirements of a service. For example, an in-memory database service can be deployed on EC2 Memory-optimized instances and the service for CPU-intensive image processing can be deployed on EC2 Compute-optimized instances.

- Reusable Code. Separating software into small, well-defined components enables teams to utilize functions for several purposes. A service created for a specific function can be utilized as a foundation for another feature. With this, an application can bootstrap off itself, since developers can build new capabilities without having to write code from scratch.

- The Microservices architecture pattern allows the independent deployment of each microservice. It makes continuous deployment possible. Developers never have to coordinate deployment for changes specific to their service. You can deploy changes like this after they have been tested.

- Microservice architecture allows the independent deployment of each microservice by a team that is dedicated to that service. Developers are allowed to choose any appropriate technology, as long as the service fulfills the API contract. Obviously, most companies would want to prevent total chaos by limiting technology choices. However, this autonomy signifies that developers are not obligated to utilize the obsolete technologies that were present at the beginning of a project. Developers have the choice of using current technology when creating a new service. Moreover, since services are quite small it becomes possible to rewrite an outdated service using current technology.

- It tackles the issue of complexity. It breaks down a huge monolithic application into a group of services. While there is no change in the total functionality amount, the application has been decomposed into manageable services or components. Each service has a distinct boundary, represented by a message-driven or RPC-driven API. The Microservices architecture pattern implements a standard of modularity that is very hard to accomplish with a monolithic codebase. As a result, it is much faster to develop individual services, and much easier to maintain and understand them.

- It eliminates technology or vendor lock-in. Microservices offer the flexibility to test new technology stacks on individual services when required. There will not be as many dependency problems and it becomes much easier to roll back changes. With less code involved, there is more flexibility.

- It complements cloud activities.
- Better fault isolation; if a single microservice fails, the remaining will continue to work.
- Components can be distributed across several servers or even several data centers.
- Functions properly with containers, like Docker.

Challenges of Microservices

Below are the drawbacks associated with implementing microservices:

- It can be challenging to deploy a microservices-based application. For a monolithic application, you simply deploy it on a group of identical servers that are behind a standard load-balancer. All application instances are configured with the locations (ports and hosts) of infrastructure services. On the other hand, a microservice application usually have a substantial number of services, and each service will have numerous runtime instances. That involves several more moving parts that have to be monitored, scaled, deployed, and configured. Additionally, a service discovery mechanism – allows a service to find the locations (ports and hosts) of all the services it needs to interact with – will need to be implemented. A high automation level and greater control of deployment techniques by developers will assist in the successful deployment of a microservices application.

- It can be challenging to test a microservices-based application. For instance, using a modern framework like Spring Boot it is easy to create a test class that launches a monolithic web application, in addition to testing its REST API. On the other hand, the same test class for services would have to start up the specific service as well as any other service that it relies on (or at least develop stubs for those services).

- It can be challenging to develop distributed systems. Developers need to select and execute an inter-process communication mechanism that is based on either RPC or messaging. In addition, they must write code to manage partial failure because a request's destination might be unavailable or slow. Even though this is not a difficult thing to do, it is more complex than what occurs in a monolithic application wherein modules invoke each other through procedure calls or language-level method.

- It is a bit challenging to implement changes that span across multiple services. For instance, assuming you are executing a story that requires updates to services X, Y, and Z, where X relies on Y and Y relies on Z. If this were a monolithic application, the corresponding modules will be changed, the changes integrated, and deployed all at once. Meanwhile, for a microservices-based application, the rollout of changes to every individual service have to be coordinated and carefully planned. For instance, service Z will be updated first, followed by service Y, and then finally service X. Fortunately, most changes typically affect only a single service and multi-service changes requiring coordination are relatively uncommon.

Relationship to Containers

Containers and microservices allow developers to easily manage and build self-healing microservice-based applications. Containers provide a standard approach to package your application's dependencies, configurations, and code into one object. Containers run as resource-isolated processes and share an operating system that is installed on the server, ensuring consistent, reliable, and quick deployments, regardless of environment. An application's services can be placed inside containers that have the smallest executables and libraries needed by that application or service, thus each container can become a self-contained package. Docker is a tool that offers an easy way to test, share, and create container images, and it has turned out to be very popular among companies that have committed to building software using containers. Even though an application inside one container operates independently from applications in other containers, it will still respond to instructions from the kernel or any other orchestration tool. These orchestration tools are necessary for managing large numbers of containers. Even though Docker is capable of orchestration, several operations and development professionals prefer Kubernetes (an open-source tool for orchestrating the operations of numerous containers).

Microservices can be built without using containers. However, most companies that adopt microservices architectures will realize that containers are a more appropriate way to execute their applications.

Relationship to SOA

SOA services are administered in the company by a registry that is structured like a directory listing. Applications have to search for the services within the registry and then invoke the service. On the other hand, microservices is a type of service-oriented architecture style where applications are designed as a group of different smaller services rather than one application or software. A detailed comparison between microservices and SOA is shown below:

Criterion	Microservices	SOA
Nature of the application	Full stack in nature.	Monolithic in nature.
Remote services	Most microservice architectures depend on two protocols – simple messaging (MSMQ, JMS) and REST, and the protocol found here is typically homogeneous.	SOA architectures rely on messaging (MSMQ, AMQP) and SOAP as main remote access protocols.

Criterion	Microservices	SOA
Technology stack	The technology stack could be huge.	Lower technology stack (compared to Microservice).
Deployment	Deployment is less time-consuming and straightforward.	The deployment process is time-consuming.
Component sharing	Microservice architecture tries to reduce sharing through "bounded context." This has to do with coupling components and their data as one unit with very few dependencies.	Enterprise services are all about component sharing. SOA improves component sharing. Systems built on SOA have the possibility of being slower than systems built on microservice architecture because SOA depends on multiple services to satisfy a

Criterion	Microservices	SOA
		business request.
Design type	It is an execution of SOA.	Software features are exposed to external users as services.
Cost-effectiveness	Less cost-effective.	More cost-effective.
Dependency	Microservice application components are independent.	Business units are dependent.
Scalability	Highly scalable.	Less scalable when compared to microservices.
Heterogeneous interoperability	Microservice architecture attempts to make the architecture pattern simpler by minimizing the number of options for integration. Microservices are a better option if all your	SOA encourages the propagation of numerous heterogeneous protocols via its messaging middleware component. SOA is a better option if you would prefer to integrate

Criterion	Microservices	SOA
	services can be exposed and accessed via same remote access protocol.	multiple systems using various protocols within a heterogeneous environment.
Software size	The software size is constantly small in Microservices.	Software size is more than any traditional software.
API layer vs Middleware	The microservices architecture pattern has an API layer that is between service consumers and services.	SOA contains a messaging middleware component. This messaging middleware provides a host of supplementary capabilities not found in microservice architectures, including protocol transformation, message, message

Criterion	Microservices	SOA
		enhancement, and mediation and routing.
Focus	They are built to implement a single business task.	SOA applications are designed to perform several business tasks.

Chapter 2

Microservices Tools

Wide ranges of tools are available for supporting the creation of microservice architectures. Some of these tools are discussed below:

Programming Languages

- **<u>Spring Boot</u>:** This is a utility built over the Spring platform. Spring Boot makes it possible to create stand-alone Spring applications with minimal configuration. It saves time by automatically configuring third-party libraries and Spring. Utilizing Spring Boot is a very popular approach to building microservices in Java. Other microservice frameworks to use on the Java platform include Vert.x, Play framework, Swagger, Spark framework, Restlet framework, JHipster, and Dropwizard.

- **<u>Elixir</u>:** Expand your programming range with Elixir; a general-purpose, concurrent, functional programming language that operates on the Erlang VM.

Orchestration

- **<u>Kubernetes</u>:** This is an open-source orchestration or container management tool. Kubernetes' container management functionalities include container load-balancing, descaling and scaling of containers, and container deployment.
- **<u>Istio</u>:** This supports the deployment of services on Kubernetes. You can add manageability, security, and reliability to microservices communications via Istio's service mesh technology. This technology allows you to enhance the interactions and relationships between applications and microservices.

Serverless

- **AWS Lambda:** This tool offers infrastructure-less servers for building microservices, and charges users on a pay-per-use rate. AWS Lambda can be used together with AWS API Gateway in order to host an API or REST service. It enables your API to serve all requests made by users.

- **IronFunctions:** This is an open source Functions-as-a-Service or serverless platform that can be run anywhere. It supports functions in multiple languages and is written on Golang. AWS Lambda format is supported, and functions can be directly imported from Lambda and used as needed.

- **Claudia:** This is a serverless tool utilized for deployments for API Gateway and AWS Lambda. It automates error-prone configuration and deployment tasks. It also have tools such as Claudia API Builder and Claudia Bot Builder.

Messaging

- **RabbitMQ:** This makes use of patterns for communications between microservices and also for scaling applications concurrently. With RabbitMQ, microservices can be connected to each other to resolve the challenges of distributed systems. In addition, this tool can be used for exchanging events between individual services.

- **Apache Kafka:** This is a distributed streaming system that was initially developed at LinkedIn and came under the Apache project afterward. By design, it is distributed, agile, and scalable. It can be used for publishing and subscribing to messages.

API Testing and Management

- **<u>API Fortress</u>:** This is an API health and testing tool that automates the process of functional testing, health monitoring, and load testing. This tool is built around current API architectural practices and patterns, and is code-free.

- **<u>Postman</u>:** This tool allows you to easily implement UI-driven API tests. It makes it easy to explore RESTful API resources.

General Testing

- **<u>Gatling</u>:** This is a very capable load testing tool that is written in Scala. It can used for performance testing of microservices.

- **<u>Pact</u>:** This is a contract-testing tool and used to make sure that services can communicate with one another.

- **<u>Hoverfly</u>:** The simulation mode of this tool may be particularly beneficial for building component tests. Hoverfly offers

JUnit integration for utilizing it within JUnit tests and a simple DSL for building simulations. It can be orchestrated through JUnit's @Rule.

Other Tools

- **Hystrix:** This is a java library for fault tolerance. It is used to separate points-of-access to 3rd-party libraries, systems, and remote services within a distributed environment. It improves the entire system by separating the failing services and stopping the cascading result of failures.

- **Docker:** This open-source project enables the creation, deployment and running of applications through the use of containers. By utilizing these containers, an application can be run as a single package, and this can also include libraries and other dependencies.

- **WireMock:** This is a library for mocking and stubbing web services. It can be used for testing Microservices.

Chapter 3

Microservices Patterns

The objective of microservices has to do with increasing the rate of application releases, by breaking down the application into small individualized services, which can be deployed separately. A microservices architecture also have some challenges. These challenges can be mitigated by the design patterns discussed in subsequent paragraphs. There are five main design patterns, with each having a number of patterns under it, these categories are: cross-cutting concern patterns, observability patterns, database patterns, integration patterns, and decomposition patterns.

Cross-Cutting Concern Patterns

Blue-Green Deployment Pattern

In microservice architecture, a single application can have several microservices. If we deploy an improved version of the services after stopping every single one of the services, there will be a significant downtime that will affect the business. It will also be a nightmare to roll-back the changes. The use of the blue-green deployment pattern will avoid these issues.

This pattern can be executed to remove or reduce downtime. The blue-green deployment approach accomplishes this by running two similar production environments, identified as Green and Blue. Assuming that Green is the current production instance and Blue is the version of the application with the new updates. Only a single environment is live at any time, where the live environment serves every production traffic. Every cloud framework provide options for executing a blue-green deployment.

Circuit Breaker Pattern

Usually, a service makes a call to other services to get data, but there is the possibility of the downstream service being down. There are a couple challenges with this: to start with, the request will keep getting directed to the service that is down, hence, slowing performance and exhausting network resources. Additionally, the user experience would be unpredictable and bad.

The consumer should call a remote service through a proxy that acts in the same way as an electrical circuit breaker. If the number of continuous failures crosses the limit, the circuit breaker gets tripped, and for the span of a specified timeout period, every attempt to call the remote service will instantly fail. After the timeout ends, the circuit breaker permits a limited amount of test requests to go through. If those requests are successful, the circuit breaker restarts its usual operation.

Otherwise, if a failure occurs, the timeout period starts again. This pattern is appropriate for preventing an application from making an attempt to access a shared resource or invoke a remote service if it is highly likely for this operation to fail.

Service Discovery Pattern

In microservices, we have to address some issues when it comes to calling services. Container technology enables the dynamic allocation of IP addresses to service instances. Whenever the address changes, there is a possibility of the consumer service breaking and needing manual updates. Each service URL must be tightly coupled and remembered by the consumer.

A service registry have to be built, which will retain the metadata of every producer service as well as the specification for each one. When starting, a service instance have to register on the registry and must de-register when it is shutting down. The service discovery pattern have two types: server-side discovery and client-side discovery.

- **Server-Side Discovery Pattern**

  Here, the client invokes a service through a load-balancer. This load-balancer searches through the service registry and directs each request to a service instance that is available. Service instances are deregistered and registered with the service registry.

  One instance of a server-side discovery tool is AWS Elastic Load Balancer (ELB). An ELB is typically utilized to load-balance outside traffic from the internet. Nonetheless, you can also make use of an ELB to load-balance traffic from an internal virtual private cloud. A client creates requests (TCP or HTTP) through the ELB by making use of its DNS name. ELB load-balances the traffic across a group of registered Amazon EC2 Container Service (ECS) containers or EC2 instances. There is not an independent service registry. Rather, ECS containers and EC2 instances are registered within the ELB itself.

Another example include load-balancers and HTTP servers such as NGINX and NGINX Plus. Consul Template can be used to dynamically reverse proxy NGINX. It is a tool that regularly regenerates arbitrary configuration files that is gotten from configuration data saved within the Consul service registry. Consul Template runs a shell command whenever there is a change in the files. It creates an nginx.conf file that configures the reverse-proxying, after which it runs a command that instructs

NGINX to load the configuration again. A more advanced implementation can dynamically reconfigure NGINX Plus utilizing either its DNS or HTTP API.

Some deployment environments like Marathon and Kubernetes run a proxy on every host within the cluster. The proxy acts as the load-balancer for server-side discovery. In order to invoke a service, a client directs the request through the proxy utilizing the service's assigned port and the host's IP address. Then, the proxy forwards the request to a service instance that is available and running somewhere within the cluster.

There are several advantages and disadvantages to the server-side discovery pattern. An advantage is that there is an abstraction of discovery details from the client. Clients just invokes the load-balancer. This removes the need to apply discovery logic for every framework and programming language utilized by your service clients. In addition, some deployment environments freely offer this functionality. However, there is a drawback to this pattern. Unless the load-balancer is offered by the deployment environment, the load-balancer will be just another highly available system feature that needs to be built and managed.

- **<u>Client-Side Discovery Pattern</u>**
When making use of this pattern, the client is tasked with determining the network address of service instances that are available and load-balancing requests across the instances. The client searches through a service registry that is a database of useable service instances. Then, the

client makes use of a load-balancing algorithm to choose one of the useable service instances and generates a request.

During start up, the service instance's network address is registered on the service registry. When the instance terminates, it is eliminated from the service registry. Usually, the registration of the service instance is refreshed periodically utilizing a heartbeat mechanism. One instance of the client-side discovery tool is Netflix OSS. Its service registry is Netflix Eureka. It offers a REST API for querying available instances and for managing service-instance registration. Netflix Ribbon is one IPC client that operates with Eureka to load-balance requests across the useable service instances.

There are several advantages and disadvantages of the client-side discovery pattern. This pattern is fairly simple and, apart from the service registry, no other feature exist. Also, since the client is aware of the useable service instances, the client can make application-specific, intelligent load-balancing decisions like consistently using hashing. A disadvantage of this pattern involves the coupling of the service registry and the client. You must execute the logic for client-side service discovery for every framework and programming language utilized by your service clients.

- **The Service Registry**
  This is a key aspect of service discovery. The service registry is a database that contains the network addresses of service instances. It have to be up-to-date and highly available. Clients can cache network

address gotten from the service registry. But yet, that information ultimately becomes outdated and clients become unable to find service instances. Therefore, a service registry is made up of a collection of servers that utilize a replication protocol to sustain consistency.

As previously mentioned, one instance of a service registry is Netflix Eureka. It offers a REST API for querying and registering service instances. Service instances use POST requests to register network addresses. Every 30 seconds, the registration gets refreshed through the use of a PUT request. This registration can be removed by either the expiration of the instance registration or by utilizing an HTTP DELETE request. A client can obtain the registered service instances through the usage of an HTTP GET request.

High availability is achieved by running Eureka servers in every availability zone of the Amazon EC2 framework. Every Eureka server operates on an EC2 instance which has an Elastic IP address. The Eureka cluster configuration are stored using DNS TEXT records. This configuration contains a map from a list of network addresses to availability zones of Eureka servers. After a Eureka server is started, it queries DNS to obtain the configuration of the Eureka cluster, finds its peers, and allots itself an unutilized Elastic IP address.

Eureka service clients and services query DNS to find the network address of Eureka servers. Clients choose to utilize a Eureka server within similar availability zone. But if there is none available, the client makes use of an Eureka server in a different availability zone. Other instances of service registries include: Apache Zookeeper, Consul, and etcd. Also, some systems like AWS, Marathon, and Kubernetes do not have an straightforward service registry. Rather, the service registry is only a built-in feature of the infrastructure.

- **<u>Service Registration Method</u>**
  There are two ways to manage the deregistration and registration of service instances. These are the third-party registration pattern, and the self-registration pattern.

  With third-party registration pattern, there is no responsibility for the service instances to register on the service registry themselves. Rather, another system component referred to as the service registrar, manages the registration. This service registrar tracks updates to the group of running service instances by either subscribing to events or polling the deployment environment. When the service registrar notices a newly unused service instance it automatically registers the instance on the service registry. It also deregisters stopped service instances.

With self-registration pattern, the responsibility for deregistering and registering service instances on the service registry lies entirely on service instances themselves. Also, if needed, a service instance issues heartbeat requests to stop its registration from expiring.

External Configuration

This allows an application to operate in several environments (e.g. production, test, development) without any alterations within the application itself. Assuming you want to update the configuration of a microservice that have been reproduced about fifty times (that is, about fifty running processes). If the microservice and its configuration are packaged together, you will have to redeploy every one of the fifty instances. This can lead to some instances making use of the previous configuration, and some making use of the new one, sooner or later. Besides, sometimes microservices utilize external connections which, for instance, require passwords, usernames, and URLs. It would be beneficial to have this configuration distributed across services, if there's need to update these settings.

Externalized configuration works by saving the configuration data in an external store, like environment variables, a file system, or a database. The configuration is gotten from the external store at startup. During runtime, microservices offer an option to load the configuration again without needing to restart the service. There are several ways to apply externalized configuration. Spring Cloud and Netflix's Archaius provide well-tested and ready-to-use solutions. Cloud services like Kubernetes and AWS also provide similar services.

Chapter 4

Microservices Patterns: Observability Patterns

This is a measure of the accuracy of a system's internal state inferred from insight on its external outputs. Observability is essential nowadays, especially after considering the characteristics and the rate at which modern applications are delivered, as well as the move towards dynamic microservice architectures and containerized workloads. Therefore, it's vital that modern tools are capable of understanding an application's properties and performance. Some of the implementation of the observability pattern include conducting health checks, distributed tracing, performance metrics, and log aggregation.

Health Check

After executing a microservice architecture, there is a possibility that an available service might not be capable of handling transactions. Each service should have an endpoint that can be used to verify the application's health, for example /health endpoint. This API should be able to verify the host's status, connection to other infrastructure or services, and any specified logic.

Distributed Tracing

This is a method utilized to monitor and profile applications, particularly those built with a microservices architecture. It assists in pinpointing what causes poor performance and where failures occur. Distributed tracing requires that software developers add instrumentation on application code. That instrumentation supplies information for the administrator to analyze performance and for the developer to debug the activities of complex software.

Distributed tracing depends on spans and traces. A trace is the full processing of a request. It represents the entire request's journey as it goes across all of the components or services of a distributed system. Every trace event that is generated by a request have a trace ID which tools use to search for, filter, and organize specific traces. Every trace is made up of numerous spans. A span, sometimes referred to as segment, is the operation or activity that occurs within individual components or services of the distributed system. Every span is an additional step in the complete processing of the entire request. Spans are usually timed and named operations. They each have a distinct span ID, and can also have metadata or other annotations.

Operations staff and software developers can trace a request from a user across each span, correlate every span to a specific service instance, and even identify the host system's physical address on which each span implements. The spans create a complete view of the request trace. It is possible to identify the source of an issue by evaluating each span that is within a trace. Trace data is not processed and shared in real time. Instead, it is produced and stored in local storage resources through the use of daemons or agents that communicate with the application's instrumentation. Then, that data is transferred to a central location, where it is analyzed as needed. This is similar to present-day event logging and other related metrics-gathering operations. Since every distributed request trace is supposed to reflect the entire journey of a request across the application, it is typically an evaluation of end-to-end performance: starting from the period a request reaches the front-end via middleware, to back-end access and results returned to the requester. The concept of a localized trace usually does not apply to distributed request tracing operations.

Some popular tools used for distributed request tracing include the LightStep monitoring service that emerged from Google's Dapper research, X-Ray service offered by AWS, Envoy proxy tool, Zipkin (also emerged from Google's Dapper research), and Datadog.

Performance Metrics

When there's an increase in the service portfolio as a result of a microservice architecture, it gets imperative to pay attention to the transactions in order to monitor patterns and send alerts when a problem occurs. A metrics service is needed to collect statistics about individual activities. It should aggregate an application service's metrics, which provides alerting and reporting. There are a couple approaches for aggregating metrics:

- **Pull** — the metrics service is used to pull metrics from the application service. An example is Prometheus.
- **Push** — the application service pushes metrics onto the metrics service. Examples include AppDynamics and NewRelic.

Log Aggregation

Assuming there's a use case wherein an application contains multiple services, requests regularly span numerous service instances, and every service instance creates a log file that has a standardized format. There would be need for a centralized logging service which aggregates logs from every service instance. Users can analyze and search the logs. They can set up alerts that are generated when certain messages show up in the logs. For instance, Pivotal Cloud Foundry (PCF) have a log aggregator that collects logs from applications and every component (diego, controller, router etc.) of the PCF framework. Another example is AWS Cloud Watch which operates the same way.

Chapter 5

Microservices Patterns: Database Patterns

When describing microservices' database architecture, the following points have to be considered: different services have several data storage requirements; databases must sometimes be shared and replicated in order to scale; some business transactions have to search through data owned by numerous services; business transactions might apply invariants that span numerous services; services should be loosely-coupled. They can be independently built, deployed, and scaled.

Saga Pattern

A saga is a series of local transactions. Every service in a saga carries out its own transaction and generates an event. The remaining services receive that event and carry out the next local transaction. When one transaction fails for any reason, the saga also implements compensating transactions to reverse the impact of the previous transactions. The saga pattern have two approaches: orchestration and choreography.

In the orchestration approach, a Saga orchestrator handles all the transactions and instructs the participant services to implement local transactions that are based on events. This Saga orchestrator is also known as Saga Manager. This orchestrator handles failure recovery by implementing compensating transactions, executes Saga requests by communicating to other services, and stores and interprets the state machine. State machines are composed of several states, with each performing a particular task. The state machine transfers data between components, and determines the subsequent step in the application's operations. This approach is used when there is control over every actor in the process, when all these actors are in a single domain of control, when there is control over the flow of activities, and when there is control over the organization where the specified business process is implemented.

In the choreography approach, there is no main orchestrator. Every service within the Saga publish events and executes their transaction. The other services implement those events and carry out their transactions. Some other events may or may not be published depending on the situation. Choreography approach specifies how more than one participants – none of which can control or have visibility over the processes of the other participants — can coordinate their processes and operations to share value and information. This approach can be utilized when there is a requirement for coordination across domains of visibility/control. It is similar to a network protocol. It specifies acceptable patterns of responses and requests between participants.

Event Sourcing

Most applications operate with data, and the usual approach is that the application maintains its current state. For instance, in the typical CRUD model a traditional data process reads data directly from the store. The Event Sourcing pattern describes a way to handle data operations that is driven by a series of events, with each of them saved in an append-only store. The application code publishes a sequence of events – that essentially define each action taken on the data – toward the event store, wherein they are persisted. Every event represents a group of changes on the data (for example, updating the cart in an online store).

These events are saved in an event store, which represents the system of record. Normal usage of the events published through the event store include maintaining materialized views of entities just as actions within the application, and for integration with other systems. For instance, a system can retain a materialized view of every customer order utilized to populate areas of the user interface. As the application updates shipping information, and removes or update items on the order, the events that define these changes can be managed and utilized to modify the materialized view.

Database-Per-Service

Here, each microservice handles its own data. This means that the data can't be directly accessed by any other microservice. Exchange or communication of data can only occur through the usage of a collection of properly-defined APIs. It sounds simpler than it really is to execute this pattern. Usually, microservices require data from each other to implement their logic. This results in interactions between several services within your application.

For this pattern to be successful, there have to be an effective definition of your application's bounded contexts. It is simpler to do this for a new system or application, but troublesome for an existing large application. Other challenges include executing business transactions that span numerous microservices, and executing queries that are supposed to expose data from more than one different bounded contexts. Nonetheless, if done properly, the main benefits of this pattern include loose coupling between microservices. Also, the microservices can be individually scaled up. It can enable the developers to select a particular database solution for a specified microservice.

Shared Database

If the challenges around Database-Per-Service gets very difficult for your team to handle, a viable option could be using a shared database. This approach attempts to solve the same issues. But it does this by implementing a far more lenient approach through the usage of a shared database that is accessed by numerous microservices. This is mostly a pattern that is safer for developers since they can work with existing ways. ACID transactions are made use of to enforce consistency.

However, the shared database approach diminishes most of the advantages of microservices. Developers across several teams have to coordinate for schema updates to tables. Also, run-time conflicts occur when multiple services are attempting to access similar database resources. In general, this approach have more disadvantages than advantages in the long run.

Command Query Responsibility Segregation (CQRS)

This pattern suggests dividing the application into two sections —the query side and the command side. The command side handles the requests that include creating updating, and deletions. The query side manages the query part by utilizing the materialized views. This pattern is mostly used together with the event sourcing pattern to generate events for all data changes. The subscription to the sequence of events keeps materialized views updated.

In CQRS, an application subscribes to domain events from different microservices and query the database or update the view. Complex aggregation queries can be served from this database. Accordingly, microservices can be scaled up and performance optimized. The disadvantage of this approach involves an increase in complexity and code duplication. This can lead to latency issues wherein the view database is ultimately consistent instead of being continuously consistent.

Chapter 6

Microservices Patterns: Integration Patterns

Client-Side UI Composition Pattern

Developing services by breaking down subdomains or business capabilities have the services that are responsible for user experience pulling data from multiple microservices. In monolithic architecture, only one call is made from the user interface to the backend service to obtain data and submit/refresh the user interface. However, it won't be the same with a microservices architecture.

With microservices, the user interface should be developed as a skeleton with numerous regions/sections of the page/screen. Every section makes a call to a separate backend microservice to retrieve the data. Frameworks such as ReactJS and AngularJS help to easily achieve that. These screens/pages are called Single Page Applications (SPA). Every team creates a client-side UI component, like an AngularJS directive, which implements the sections of the page for a specified service. A user interface development team is responsible for executing the page skeletons that create screens/pages by composing numerous, service-specific UI components.

Aggregator Pattern

When decomposing business functionality into multiple smaller logical parts of code, it becomes essential to contemplate on how to coordinate the data returned by every service. The Aggregator pattern assists in addressing this. It is about aggregating data from various services and then sending the final response back to the consumer. Aggregator pattern can be implemented in two ways: An API Gateway partitions the request into numerous microservices and collects the data before it is sent to the consumer; A composite microservice invokes the necessary microservices, combines the data, and converts the data before it is sent back. A composite microservice is recommended if applying any business logic, else, API Gateway is the standard solution.

Chained Microservice Design Pattern

This pattern generates a single integrated response to a request. In this situation, Service A receives a request from the client, which is then redirected to Service B, which may redirect it again. Every service probably makes use of a synchronous HTTP response/request messaging. The client is blocked till the entire chain of response/request is finished. It is necessary for the chain not to be too long, since the chain's synchronous nature will look like a long wait on the client side, particularly if it's a webpage waiting to display the response. A chain with one microservice is known as singleton chain and this may permit the chain to be expanded at a later point.

Branch Pattern

This pattern extends the aggregator pattern. With branch pattern, you can concurrently process the response and request from two separate or to be exact, two mutually exclusive microservices chains. The branch pattern also provides flexibility to summon separate numerous chains or even one chain in accordance with the business requirements. For web applications or eCommerce websites, there may be a need to get data from several sources belonging to various microservices. Branch pattern plays an efficient role here.

Gateway Routing Pattern

This pattern routes requests to numerous services through a single endpoint. It is useful when you want to expose several services on one endpoint and forward to the appropriate service depending on the request. The client application only have to communicate with and know about one endpoint. If a service gets decomposed or consolidated, the client does not really require updating. Requests will still be sent to the gateway, just the routing changes. Also, gateway routing pattern permits the abstraction of backend services from clients, enabling you to keep calls to the client simple while allowing changes to the backend services that is behind the gateway.

Proxy Pattern

This is a variation of aggregator pattern. In this instance, no aggregation needs to occur on the client instead a separate microservice may be invoked depending on the business requirement. This pattern can be used when there is no need to expose every service to the consumer, rather have all the services go through an interface. If the proxy is a dumb proxy, the request is delegated to one of the available services. Alternatively, if it is a smart proxy, the data is first transformed before sending the response to the client. Proxy pattern can scale independently on Z-axis and X-axis as well.

API Gateway Pattern

Fetching data from all running services is vital for any application. In the microservice architecture, it is essential to retrieve the data from separate services. However, it is tricky to fetch user-owned resources from the assortments of microservices provided from a single user interface since the UI captures so many information of the end user. The API gateway acts as a helpline by producing one entry-point for every interaction that happens within the architecture. It also assists in establishing security by authorizing clients and exposing important APIs in regard to the client.

Since the API gateway is a single point of contact, it can not only serve as a proxy server used to direct requests to microservices but it also collects results from numerous services and send the response back to the user. It manages multiple protocol requests and transforms data whenever required (for example, HTTPS to AMQP and backwards).

Chapter 7

Microservices Patterns: Decomposition Patterns

Sidecar Pattern

This pattern involves deploying application components into a separate container or process to provide encapsulation and isolation. The sidecar pattern also allow applications to be comprised of heterogeneous technologies and components. It is sometimes known as the sidekick pattern. This pattern is called Sidecar because it looks like a sidecar that is affixed to a motorcycle. In the sidecar pattern, the sidecar is affixed to a parent application as well as offer supporting features for that application. This pattern have the same lifecycle as the parent application, in that it is created and retired parallel to the parent.

Services and applications sometimes require related functionality, for example, networking, configuration, logging, and monitoring services. These tasks can be executed as separate services or components. If they are tightly coupled with the application, then they can operate in the same process like that of the application, making productive use of the resources that are shared. However, this also signifies that they are not properly isolated, and if one component fails, it can impact other components or the whole application. Also, they typically need to be executed using the same language like that of the parent application. Consequently, the application and the component have close interdependence with one another.

If the application is broken down into services, then every service can be built utilizing different technologies and languages.

While this offers more flexibility, it signifies that every component have its own dependencies and needs language-specific libraries to examine the underlying platform and all shared resources. Additionally, deploying these components as individual services adds latency onto the application. Also, handling the dependencies and code for these language-specific interfaces adds significant complexity, especially for management, deployment, and hosting. To resolve this complexity, co-locate a cohesive group of tasks with the main application, but place them within their own container or process, providing a consistent interface for platform services on various languages.

A sidecar pattern can be used when there is need for:

- strong control over resource restrictions for a particular component or resource. For instance, there may be a need to limit the memory amount that a specific component utilizes. The component can be deployed as a sidecar and the memory usage can be separately managed from the principal application; a service that shares the main application's overall lifecycle, but can be updated independently;

- a feature or component co-locating on the same host like the application;
- a different organization or remote team owning a component;
- a main application that uses a diverse set of frameworks and languages. A component located within a sidecar service could be consumed by applications that are written in various languages using different frameworks.

A sidecar pattern may not be appropriate:

- when the service have to scale independently from or differently than the principal applications. If this is the case, it may be more appropriate to deploy the component as a separate service;
- for small applications wherein the cost (in terms of resources) of installing a sidecar service for every instance is just not worth the benefit of isolation;
- when inter-process communication have to be improved. Communication between sidecar services and a parent application includes some overhead, especially latency in calls. This might not be a satisfactory trade-off for chatty interfaces.

Bulkhead Pattern

This pattern handles failure well. In a bulkhead architecture, features of an application are separated into pools such that if one feature fails, the other features will continue to work. It's named after the partitioned sections (bulkheads) of the hull of a ship. If the ship's hull is compromised, only the destroyed section fills with water, thus preventing the ship from sinking.

The advantages of this pattern include:

- it allows the deployment of services that provide a different service quality for consuming applications. You can configure a high-priority consumer pool to utilize high-priority services;
- it allows the preservation of some functionality in case a service fails. Other features and services of the application will keep working;
- it isolates services and consumers from cascading failures. A problem affecting a service or consumer can be isolated inside

its own bulkhead, stopping the whole solution from failing.

Strangler Pattern

This pattern is used to incrementally transform monolithic application to microservices by replacing a specific functionality with a new service. After the new functionality is available, the old feature gets strangled, the new service is utilized, and the old feature is decommissioned altogether. New developments are done on the new service, rather than the monolith. This enables you to attain high-quality code development for greenfield.

The steps of the Strangler Application include transform, coexist, and eliminate. In the transform step, a parallel new site is created (for instance, in IBM Cloud or in your current environment but using more modern approaches). When in the coexist step, leave the current site at its current location for a specific period. Redirect from the current site to the new site so the functionality is executed incrementally. When in the eliminate step, the old functionality should be removed from the current site (or simply end its maintenance) as traffic is routed away from that part of the old site.

Two-Phase Commit Protocol (2PC)

This is a mechanism for executing a transaction across various software components (multiple message queues, databases etc.). The transaction coordinator is one of the vital participants within a distributed transaction. The distributed transaction have two phases, which are the Prepare phase, and the Rollback or Commit phase. In the Prepare phase, all transaction participants prepare for commit and broadcast to the coordinator their readiness to complete the transaction. In the Rollback or Commit phase, the transaction coordinator issues either a rollback or a commit command to all participants.

The advantages of this approach include: it is a synchronous call, wherein the client would be informed of failure or success; it facilitates read-write isolation, updates on objects are not noticeable until the changes are committed by the transaction coordinator; it guarantees the atomicity of transactions . The transaction ends with either every microservice being successful or have nothing changed in all microservices.

There are drawbacks to this approach. 2PC protocol is quite slow when compared to the time of operation for a single microservice. It relies heavily on the transaction coordinator, leading to the system slowing down during high load. Locking of database rows is another drawback. The lock could turn out to be a performance bottleneck, with the possibility of resulting in a deadlock, where a couple transactions mutually lock one another.

Decompose by Subdomain

A domain has to do with real-world features of a solution (for example, content management, retail loans, banking, mortgage, etc.) The domain describes the acceptance criteria and requirements for the system that will be created by the developer; it can be looked at as a very high-level type of segregation for various areas of the business. A domain can be broken down into subdomains, and this is one specific part of the domain. Usually, a subdomain reflect some organizational structure wherein some users use a particular ubiquitous language.

For instance, banking can be decomposed into investment management, account management, payments, investment management, and cards; where cards itself can further be broken down to merchant relations, card payments, card billing, and card authorization.

Subdomains can be categorized as generic, supporting, and core. Subdomains in the generic category are not particular to the business and ideally are executed using off-the-shelf software. Subdomains in the supporting category are associated with business operations but are not differentiators. They can be outsourced or implemented in-house. Subdomains in the core category are vital differentiators for the business and very valuable aspects of the application.

The characteristics of subdomains include:

- every domain can be structured into subdomains;
- every subdomain can have further subdomains;
- there can be communication amongst various subdomains;
- typical Black-and-Whitebox modelling;
- mapping applications to subdomains and domain is a traditional enterprise architecture approach.

Decompose by Business Capability

A business capability refers to a structured modelling that offers a high-level view of the business. It is at the top area of the business architecture. The microservices approach uses a business model's capabilities to modularize services. A monolithic application can be split into services by using business capabilities. The services created this way have broad context boundaries.

For example, in every company, there are several departments that work collaboratively to get things done. These include maintenance, service, sales, marketing, and technical. To visualize a microservice structure, each of these various domains would be the microservices while the company will be the system.

Chapter 8

Testing Microservices

The combination of a container-based infrastructure and microservice architectural style requires a compatible testing strategy. A microservice architecture depends more on remote dependencies and depend less on in-process features, and your test environments and testing strategy have to adapt to these alterations. More over-the-wire communication leads to extra effort spent testing the contracts and connections between your microservices. Also, multiple new testing strategies are available to manage dependent components when migrating to a container-based architecture, which often occurs when implementing microservices. Testing techniques should be chosen with a perspective on risk, cost, and time to market.

You will be using several of the same testing strategies used for monolithic architectures in addition to new techniques involving containers. Besides, there may be a change in the suitability of different testing strategies, because of the microservice architecture's tighter feedback loops since teams are typically cross-functional and co-located. Now it's time we examine some approaches to automated testing of microservices.

Contract Testing

This is important when using loosely-coupled components such as microservices. A contract defines how components interact and communicate with each other, behavioral considerations of components (semantics) as well as message formats amongst components (syntax). Contract testing is used to guarantee the fulfillment of contracts between components; this gives the assurance that the components are capable of working together. When using test-specific dependent components (like test doubles), contract testing can also be used to ensure that they fulfill the latest or any particular version of the contract.

Pact is an example of a tool that can be utilized for contract testing. Contract testing certifies that services can interact with each other without executing integration tests. The contract is signed between both sides of communication: provider and consumer. Pact supposes that contract code is created and published on the side of the consumer, and then certified by the provider. Pact offers a tool that shares and stores the contracts between providers and consumers. It is known as Pact Broker. It delivers a straightforward RESTful API for retrieving and publishing pacts, as well as an embedded online

dashboard for navigating through the API.
Pact Broker can be easily run on the local
system using its Docker image.

Below are several ways of managing or testing
contracts between components:

- **<u>End-to-end (E2E) testing</u>** suggests
  verifying that all components function well
  together for complete customer journeys.
  This suggests that contracts between
  components are completely validated when
  applying the user journey tests all through
  the system.
- Use contract testing for releases of
  independent component if there's a need to
  independently release a couple dependent
  components. Try to test combinations of
  production and the latest artifacts.
- **<u>Per-contract narrow integration
  testing</u>** examines the contract between the
  dependent component and the connector

module within your microservice. In this case, the contract is usually more producer driven instead of consumer driven.

- **Consumer-driven contract testing** is part of a full microservice testing technique. Consumer-driven contracts are divided into consumers and a producer. Consumer-driven contract testing guarantees that the producer offers a contract that meets all consumers' expectations. Consumers confirm that the producers still offer the structure of behavior and messages they need.

- In **contract snapshot testing**, test doubles serves as an overview of a contract between components during a specific period. That snapshot can become outdated. Contract snapshots can be tested in an automated manner.

- **Contract snapshot refreshes** enables you to recreate the contracts between components. Normally, a refresh will handle the syntax and partially handles the contract semantics.

Testing in Isolation

Directly testing the functionality of a particular microservice in isolation is a good way to begin your test automation. This is typically done by making use of a REST API to communicate with your service and some kind of mocking to allow independent testing of the service, without any kind of integration with other services. You have to not just guarantee that the service itself is functional, but also make sure that your changes doesn't impact other teams that are consuming the service.

Unit Testing

This is the smallest independent test that can examine a piece of code that is in isolation. Unit tests can be used to examine a line of code or test several lines of code together. They tend to be very quick, and because of that, they form a very essential aspect of the feedback loop. Unit tests report failure when regression occurs. Due to its granularity, debugging and discovering the regressed code is easy, simply put, unit tests help to easily identify the part of the software that changed since the last update on the code, and where the problem is in the software. The tests' tight scope will make sure the tests do not go over the boundaries or bleed.

Unit tests are not as expensive as the other types of testing both in regards to time and cost, while testing an application built with the microservices architecture. Heavy mocking and stubbing should be avoided. Where possible and needed, the software's dependency should be called directly inside the tests. Having no/minimal mocks have a few advantages: makes tests easily understandable, and avoids complexity build-up in the tests.

Integration Testing

It's necessary to verify individually tested services. This critical aspect of microservice architecture testing depends on inter-service communications working properly. Service calls should be done with integration to other services, including success and error cases. Thus, integration testing verifies that the system is seamlessly working together and that dependencies between services are available as expected.

Best Practices for Microservices Testing

The subsequent paragraphs summarizes the best practices for successfully testing microservices.

- Utilize canary testing on new code. Make the most of all the monitoring provided by your provider and make sure that every code is well instrumented.

- Try to test across various setups. The more varied the code setups are, the greater the amount of bugs that will be discovered. This is particularly accurate for complex virtual environments wherein you may have minimal differences between various libraries and where the hardware architecture may, in spite of the virtualization tier, still have unplanned side effects.

- Don't attempt to assemble the whole microservice environment within a small test setup.

- Figure out the important links in the architecture and try to test those. For example, there's a significant link between the user interface that displays details, the user login service, and the database where those details are stored.

- Every service should be treated as a software component. Unit tests should be carried out on the service same as it would be for any code.

Chapter 9

Securing Microservices

When adopting microservices, it's critical to ensure that all of your software's security demands are fulfilled. Below are the best practices for a secure microservice architecture:

Third-Party Application Access through OAuth

Some third-party applications have to access data from various users, or incorporate data from numerous users. With OAuth, whenever a third-party application gains access to a service, the application alerts the user to permit a third-party application to utilize the corresponding access permission and generates an access token according to the user's authorizations.

For example, in GitHub, some third-party applications like Travis CI or GitBook, are integrated through GitHub and OAuth. OAuth has various authentication processes for various scenarios. In OAuth, an authorization code is utilized to request access token instead of returning the access token directly to the client from the authorization server. OAuth is designed this way in order to pass through the browser when redirecting to the callback URL of the client system. There is a risk of the access token being stolen if it is passed directly. By using an authorization code, the client interacts directly with the authorization/permission server when requesting for the access token. Also, the authorization server approves the client when handling the client's token request. This prevents others from falsifying the client's identity and using the authentication code.

When executing the user authentication for the microservice, OAuth may be utilized to delegate the microservice's user authentication onto a third-party authentication service vendor. The purpose of utilizing OAuth for user authorization of microservices and third-party application access is different. The latter is to authorize the users' private data access rights in microservices towards third-party applications. Microservices are resource and authorization servers in the OAuth framework. The purpose of the former is to utilize and integrate the OAuth authentication service offered by a well-known authentication vendor, which simplifies the complicated registration operation, in this instance the microservice assumes the client's role in the OAuth architecture. Thus, we need to differentiate between these two scenarios in order to avoid misunderstandings.

Third-Party Application Access through API Token

The third-party makes use of an API token issued by an application to gain access to the application's data. This token is produced by the user from within the application and presented to third-party applications for their use. In this case, usually third-party applications can access just the user's own token data, but not other users' confidential private data.

For instance, GitHub offers the personal API Token functionality. Users can generate a token through GitHub's developer settings interface, then utilize the token to gain access to the GitHub API. When generating a token, you can outline the token data's access right, such as updating user information, viewing user information, deleting Repo, viewing Repo information, and so on.

The advantage of making use of the API Token rather than directly using the username/password to gain access to the API is to minimize the risk of leaving the user's password unprotected, and to retrieve the token's permissions whenever without needing to change the password.

Distributed Session Management

To achieve the resiliency and scalability of microservices in addition to taking full advantage of the benefits offered by the microservice architecture, it is preferable for the microservices to be stateless. This approach can be applied via different ways such as:

- **Centralized Session Storage**
  This implies that when a user gains access to a microservice, the user's data will be retrieved from a shared session storage, thus making sure that the same session

data is read by all microservices. This technique is very good in some scenarios as the login status for the user is opaque. It is also a solution that is scalable and highly available. However, one challenge with this approach is that it requires a specific protection mechanism and thus should be accessed via a secured process.

- **Session Replication**

  This implies that each instance stores all session data, and this is synchronized across the network. The synchronization of session data leads to network bandwidth overhead. Whenever there is a change in the session data, the data would have to be synchronized to the remaining systems.

- **Sticky Session**

  This ensures that every request from a particular user is routed to the same server that handled the first request from that user, thus ensuring the accuracy of session data for a specific user. However, this solution relies on the load-balancer. It can only fulfill the scenario for horizontally expanded clusters, but when (for any reason) the load-balancer is suddenly forced to move users to another server, all the session data for the users will be lost.

Single Sign-On

This is an authentication method that enables users to access numerous applications with a single set of login credentials. Here, users log in once, then gain access to various applications without having to re-enter login credentials for each application. This enables seamless network resource usage. SSO is not appropriate for systems needing guaranteed access, since the loss of login credentials leads to denial-of-access for all systems. It is preferable for SSO to be utilized with other authentication techniques, like one-time password tokens and smart cards.

Mutual Authentication

There is a huge amount of horizontal traffic amongst microservices, along with vertical traffic from third parties and users. These traffic may be across different datacenters or in same local area network. Mutual authentication between microservices is achieved through mutual SSL, and TLS can be used to encrypt data transmission between microservices.

A certificate should be generated for all microservices, and each microservice can be authenticated with certificates from the others. Within the microservice operating framework, there may be a huge amount of microservice instances, and these microservice instances often experience dynamic changes, such as the addition of service instances when the level expands. In such cases, it becomes very difficult to create and distribute certificates. A private certificate center (for example, internal PKI/CA) can be created to offer certificate management for several microservices.

Client Token

In monolithic architecture, session is used to store the user state on the server. This affects the server's horizontal expansion since the server is stateful. For microservice architecture, it is recommended to make use of token to store user login status. The main difference between session and token lies in how they are stored. Sessions are stored centrally within the server while tokens are normally stored in the browser as cookies. The token contains the user's identity information. Each time a request is conveyed to the server, it assesses the visitor's identity and determines whether the visitor is authorized to access the resource that was requested. The token is utilized to validate the user's identity. Thus, the token's content needs to be encrypted so as to avoid manipulation by a third party or the requester. JSON Web Token (JWT) is an open standard that specifies the token content, specifies the token format, encrypts it, and provides libraries for various languages. A JWT token has a very simple structure and is made up of three parts:

- **Signature**

  This is utilized by the client to validate the identity of the token and also to confirm that the content wasn't changed during transmission.

- **Payload**

  This includes standard information like the username, user id, and expiration date. It can also include user roles and user-specific information.

- **<u>Header</u>**

  This contains type and the hash algorithm utilized by JWT.

These three parts are merged using Base64 encoding to become token strings (separated by ".") that are eventually sent back to the client. By making use of token for user authentication, user status is not saved on the server. Every time a request is made by the client, it sends the token for authentication on the server.

API Gateway with Client Token

The user's authentication process is similar to the fundamental process of authenticating token. The difference here has to do with the API Gateway being added as the entry point for external requests. This implies that all requests must pass through the API gateway, successfully hiding the microservices. When requested, the API gateway converts the original user token to an opaque token that can only be resolved by it. In this case, it is not a problem to log off since the API gateway can nullify the user's token after logging off.

Private and Public APIs

APIs play an integral role in microservices, linking the various components together and permitting them to interact. There are two types of these APIs: private and public. Private APIs are those APIs that the development team utilizes within larger applications for communication between owners of various services, while public APIs are those APIs that consumers make use of to access a service or resource through an application. It is necessary to secure both private and public APIs. This can be a huge challenge due to the microservice architecture's distributed nature, and as security teams lose sight of APIs that are quickly expanding and changing.

Chapter 10

Adopting Microservices

There is no standard set of steps to follow when building a microservice architecture. However, there are some common strategies followed by many companies that adopted microservices architecture, and they used these to achieve success. Some of these common strategies include:

- ***Logging and Monitoring***
  Microservices are distributed by nature, thus it can be a challenge to log and monitor individual services. It is difficult to correlate and go through the logs of every service instance and discover individual errors. Just like with monolithic applications, microservices cannot be monitored from a single place.

To resolve such problems, a preferred strategy is to make the most of a streamlined logging service that collects logs from all service instances. Users can explore these logs from one central spot and configure alerts for certain messages. There are existing tools that are widely used by several companies. One of such is ELK Stack, which is the most frequently utilized solution where the logging daemon (Logstash), gathers and aggregate logs that are searchable through Kibana dashboard and indexed by Elasticsearch.

Another strategy is stats aggregation such as memory usage and CPU that can be leveraged and stored in a central location. Tools like Graphite perform well in pushing to and storing in a central repository efficiently. When a single downstream service is not able to handle requests, there must be a way to generate an alert. This is where implementing health-check APIs in each service gets important since they provide information on the system health. A health-check client (either a load-balancer or a monitoring service) invokes the endpoint to verify the condition of the service instance regularly within a certain time period. Even if every downstream service is healthy, there might still be a communication issue between services. Tools like Netflix's Hystrix project offers the capability to detect those types of problems.

- ***Create Standards***
  When there are several teams taking care of various services independently, it is good to introduce some best practices and standards — error handling, for instance. As might be expected, when best practices

and standards are not given, each service would probably handle errors differently, leading to the creation of a huge amount of unnecessary code. Making standards is always beneficial in the long run (for example PayPal API Style Guide). It is also essential to let others understand the functions of an API in addition to providing the documentation of the API. There are tools such as Swagger that provide support for development across the full API lifecycle, from documentation and design, to deployment and testing. Swagger enables the ability to build metadata for an API and have users play with it, thus, allowing users to further understand it and utilize it more effectively.

In a microservices architecture, after a while, each service starts gradually relying on more services. This can present more issues as the services progresses, for instance, there might be a dynamic change in the amount of service instances and locations (port number, host). The protocols and the data-sharing format might also differ from service to service. Here is where Service Discovery and API Gateways become very helpful. Executing an API Gateway becomes one entry point for every client. An API Gateways can render a different API for every client. It might also implement security, like validating that the client has the authorization to perform the request. Tools like Zookeeper can be utilized for Service Discovery (even though it was not designed for that purpose). More modern tools like HashiCorp's Consul are definitely worth exploring in regards to Service Discovery.

- **Decentralize Things**

  There are companies that implemented microservices successfully and followed a process where the teams that develop the services manage everything connected to that service. These teams are the ones that create, deploy, support, and maintain it. There are no other maintenance or support teams.

  Another way to accomplish the same has to do with having an internal open-source process. By taking this method, developers that need to update a service can get the code, make the necessary change, and submit a pull request themselves rather than waiting on the service owner to get and work on necessary changes. In order for this to work correctly, the appropriate technical documentation is required along with setup guidance and instructions for each service so as to make it easy for anyone to get the service and work on it. A hidden advantage of this method is that developers are more focused on creating high quality code since they realize that others have access to the code and will examine it.

Furthermore, some architectural patterns can assist in decentralizing things. For instance, you might build an architecture where the set of services are communicating through a central message bus. The bus manages the message routing from different services. A good example includes message brokers like RabbitMQ. What tends to happen after a while is that people start putting additional logic onto this central message bus and it begins to know more about the domain. As it gets more intelligent, that can essentially become a problem since it gets difficult to make changes, requiring collaboration across separate dedicated teams. This type of architecture should relatively be kept "dumb" – only handle message routing. Event based architectures appear to work well in scenarios like this.

- ***Build and Deploy***
  After making a decision on the service requirements of these microservices, they can be created by one or more teams using the technologies that best fits each purpose. For instance, you may decide to create a Product Service in Java with a Microsoft SQL Server database and Spark/Scala as the Product Recommendation Service. Once built, CI/CD pipelines can be configured with any of the existing CI servers (Go, TeamCity, Jenkins, etc.) to execute the automated test cases, then

deploy these services individually to different environments (production, staging, QA, integration etc.).

- *Failure*

  It is important to know that by default, microservices aren't resilient. Services might fail. Failures can occur due to failures in dependent services. Failures can also arise for a multitude of reasons like network time outs, bugs in code etc. With a microservices architecture, it is critical to make sure that the entire system does not get affected or undergo downtime when an error occurs in a separate part of the system. Patterns like Circuit Breaker or Bulkhead can assist in attaining better resiliency

  The Bulkhead pattern isolates components of an application into groups so that if one malfunctions, the others will remain functional. The pattern is named Bulkhead because it looks like the segmented sections of a ship's hull. When there is an issue with the ship's hull, only the damaged segment fills with water, preventing the ship from sinking.

The Circuit Breaker pattern encloses a protected function call within a circuit breaker object that monitors for failures. If a failure crosses the boundary, it trips the circuit breaker, and all additional calls made to the circuit breaker will return an error, with no protected call being done at all for a specified configured timeout. Once the timeout ends, some calls are allowed to pass through by the circuit breaker, and if they are successful, the circuit breaker returns to its normal state. During the time the circuit breaker failed, users are notified

that a certain section of the system has
failed and the remaining parts can still be
used. Note that it can be a multi-
dimensional task to provide the required
level of durability for an application.

- ***Breaking Down Services***
  One way to make it easier to adopt
  microservices could be to describe services
  that corresponds to business capabilities.
  Business capabilities are things a business
  does to offer value to its end-users.
  Establishing business capabilities and
  matching services requires a high-level
  comprehension of the business. For
  instance, the business capabilities for a
  sales and marketing system might include:
  commission management, campaign
  management, opportunity/lead
  management, brand management, prospect
  management, sales support, product

support, sales planning, campaign
execution, advertising, and business
development.

After identifying the business capabilities,
the needed services can be created
corresponding to each one of the described
business capabilities. Each of these services
can be maintained by a separate team that
becomes proficient in that specific domain
and proficient in the technologies that are
more appropriate for those specific
services. This often results in more stable
teams and more stable API boundaries.

- **_Deployment_**
  It is necessary to create Consumer-Driven
  Contracts for all APIs that are being relied
  on. This is to make sure that you do not
  break your API when you add new changes.
  In Consumer-Driven Contracts, every

consumer API captures what is expected of the provider within a separate contract. Every contract is shared with the provider in order for them to gain insight into the requirements they must accomplish for each individual client. Consumer-Driven Contracts must completely pass before deployment and before making any changes to the API. In addition, it assists the provider in knowing the services that depends on it and the nature of the dependence. When it comes to the deployment of independent microservices, the common models used are: multiple microservices for each operating system, and a single microservice for each operating system.

You can deploy multiple microservices for each operating system. With this approach, automating certain things saves time, for example, you don't have to provision the host for every service. The downside of this method is that it restricts the ability to scale and change services independently. It also introduces difficulty in handling dependencies. For example, all the services residing on the same host would have to use same Java version if they are developed in Java. Additionally, these independent services can create unwanted impact on other running services that can be a very challenging problem to reproduce and resolve.

Due to the above issue, the second approach, where a single microservice for each operating system is deployed, is the better choice. With this approach, there is more isolation of the service and hence it is easier to scale services and handle dependencies independently. The traditional solution for resolving this problem is through the use of Hypervisors – where multiple virtual machines are set up on the same host. Going with this approach can be costly since the hypervisor process is utilizing some resources and when more virtual machines are provisioned, there will be more resources consumed. To negate this, the use of the container model is recommended. One example of an implementation of that model is Docker.

Another common problem usually faced with a microservices approach is deciding how to modify existing microservice APIs when it is in use in production. Modifying the microservice API might disrupt the microservice that depends on it. There are several ways to solve this problem. First, version the API and when updates are needed for the API, you can deploy the API's new version while still having the first version up. You can then upgrade the dependent services to utilize the newer version. After every dependent service have been migrated to utilize the newer version of the updated microservice, the first version can be brought down. This approach has a slight problem since it becomes hard to maintain the different versions. Any bug fixes or new changes must be implemented in both versions. Due to this, an alternative method can be considered wherein another endpoint is executed in the same service that needs the changes. Once the new endpoint is being fully used by every service, then the old endpoint can be deleted. The unique advantage of this approach is that its service maintenance is easier since there

will always be just one API version
running.

- ***Carefully Design the Individual
  Services***

  When designing the services, thoroughly
  define them and consider what will be
  exposed, the protocols that will be used to
  engage with the service, and so on. It is
  very vital to hide the service's
  implementation details and any complexity
  and only expose the details required by the
  clients of the service. If you expose
  unnecessary details, it becomes very hard
  to change the service in the future, as there
  will be much painstaking work to find out
  who is depending on the various
  components of the service. Moreover, a
  great deal of agility is lost in being capable
  of deploying the service independently.

Chapter 11

Conclusion

Microservice architecture came about because the traditional way of developing enterprise applications—utilizing a monolithic method—got problematic as applications became larger and more complex. Microservices solve the challenges of monolithic applications by being modular. In the simplest form, microservices assists in building an application as a set of small services, with each service being independently deployable and operating in its own process. Containers and microservices allow developers to easily manage and build self-healing microservice-based applications. Microservice patterns are categorized under cross-cutting concern patterns, observability patterns, database patterns, integration patterns, and decomposition patterns. It is essential to test and secure the microservices architecture, applying the best practices for these will aid in an easier and safer implementation of the microservices architecture.

Other Books by Same Author

- Productive DevOps: Your Complete Handbook on Building a Dependable, Agile and Secure Organization
- Cloud Computing: A Comprehensive Guide to Cloud Computing
- Infrastructure as Code: A Comprehensive Guide to Managing Infrastructure as Code